THE GOLDEN AGE
OF AIR TRAVEL

Nina Hadaway

SHIRE PUBLICATIONS

Published in Great Britain in 2013 by Shire Publications Ltd, Midland House, West Way, Botley, Oxford OX2 0PH, United Kingdom.

4301 21st St, Suite 220B, Long Island City, NY 11101, USA.

E-mail: shire@shirebooks.co.uk   www.shirebooks.co.uk

© 2013 Nina Hadaway.

A CIP catalogue record for this book is available from the British Library.

Shire Library no. 729.   ISBN-13: 978 0 74781 223 4

Nina Hadaway has asserted her right under the Copyright, Designs and Patents Act, 1988, to be identified as the author of this book.

Designed by Tony Truscott Designs, Sussex, UK and typeset in Perpetua and Gill Sans.

Printed in China through Worldprint Ltd.

13 14 15 16 17   10 9 8 7 6 5 4 3 2 1

COVER IMAGE
1950s American advert showing passengers boarding a TWA flight.

TITLE PAGE IMAGE
View of the cockpit, captain and first officer on board a Vickers Viscount, the world's first gas-turbine-powered commercial aircraft.

CONTENTS PAGE IMAGE
Concorde in flight.

ACKNOWLEDGEMENTS
I would like to thank my family especially Stuart and Marnie for their love and support.

Images are acknowledged as follows:

Advertising Archives, cover image; Alamy, pages 16 (top), 51, 52–3 (bottom); Getty Images, page 4; The Goff family, pages 29, 36 (all), 42 (top); Imperial War Museum, pages 25, 26 (bottom), 27, 28, 39; Mary Evans, pages 10 and 14; Mirror, pages 23, 43, 46, 48 (all), 50; Peter Newark's Picture Library, pages 6, 18, 20–1 (bottom), 42 (bottom), 44 (top); RAF Museum, pages 5, 8 (all), 9 (all), 12, 13 (bottom), 20 (top), 26 (top), 30–1, 34, 41 (bottom); RAF Museum/BA Museum, cover page, contents page, pages 11, 13 (top), 16 (bottom), 17 (all), 22 (bottom), 32, 35, 37 (top right), 41 (top), 44 (bottom);

All other photographs are from the author's collection.

Shire Publications is supporting the Woodland Trust, the UK's leading woodland conservation charity, by funding the dedication of trees.

CONTENTS

INTRODUCTION 4

EARLY DAYS OF AIR TRAVEL 6

GLAMOUR AND COMFORT 14

THE WAR YEARS 24

HIGHER, FURTHER, FASTER 32

THE JET AGE 40

THE BOOM IN AIR TRAVEL 46

EPILOGUE 52

FURTHER READING 54

PLACES TO VISIT 55

INDEX 56

IMPERIAL AIRWAYS
AND ASSOCIATED COMPANIES
EUROPE · AFRICA · INDIA · CHINA · AUSTRALIA

INTRODUCTION

When once you have tasted flight you will forever walk the earth with your
eyes turned skyward… (Leonardo da Vinci)

SINCE THE DAWN OF TIME, man has turned his eyes to the sky – and
wondered. Flying has featured in fables, legends and myths. It has
become a reality through trial and error, perseverance and scientific
investigation, with the invention of both lighter-than-air vehicles such as
balloons and heavier-than-air craft. Over the years the form of these
creations has changed, with different disciplines and new technologies
coming together to determine the latest designs. The role of the aircraft
has also developed. This book looks at how commercial air travel
has evolved from short joy-rides to round-the-world flights. It highlights
the passenger experience
from the 1910s to the
1970s; a golden age of
air travel because of
the way in which flying
was undertaken, the
attitude of the public
towards flight during
this period, and the many
features that no longer
form a part of today's mass
movement of people
around the world. It
was a time when flying
was considered exciting
and modern, both a
novelty and a treat. It was
a glamorous adventure to
be savoured and enjoyed.

Opposite:
Imperial Airways
poster, 1930s.

An early woodcut
depicting the story
of Icarus flying too
close to the sun.

EARLY DAYS OF AIR TRAVEL

FLYING WAS STILL IN ITS INFANCY when the first fare-paying passengers took to the air. As early as the eighteenth and nineteenth centuries, huge crowds gathered to witness the ascents made by pioneering balloonists. Soon it became possible for members of the public to be taken up, and at the cost of a few shillings several minutes could be spent aloft.

With the development of the aeroplane, enthusiasts promoted this exciting new mode of transport. Air shows and aerial derbies were organised during the 1910s. These caught the imagination of the public, and thousands attended meetings and displays. Those held at Hendon were very popular, and the 'Hendon Habit' was formed. Attending this venue became part of the summer social calendar alongside Ascot or Henley. The pilots taking part at Hendon became celebrities and offered joy-rides that were enthusiastically taken up by those who could afford them. It became fashionable to wrap up against the elements and to go on a circuit of the showground with one of these airmen. The thrill of such an experience was often accompanied by a degree of trepidation. Lieutenant Colonel Charles Edward Stewart was a passenger at Hendon in 1912. He recalled some years later:

> There's nothing like your first flight! … I climbed … into the thing and saw my seat … was a plank with … wickerwork sides and back. The pilot's body would come between my legs and his shoulders would be level with my knees so that if the thing's nose dipped suddenly I should probably fall on top of him… I told him I felt most insecure.

The idea of taking several passengers up at once was explored, and companies such as the Grahame-White Aviation Company Ltd built aircraft for this purpose. Between 1910 and 1914 airships in Germany carried over thirty thousand passengers on sightseeing trips or on flights between the country's cities. By 1914 seasonal flights in aircraft were being undertaken in the United States and Russia. With the outbreak of the First World War, however, commercial flying in Europe effectively ceased until the conflict had ended

Opposite:
The monoplane *Atalanta*, built for the British Empire routes of Imperial Airways, flies over Croydon Airport in the 1930s. Contemporary artwork.

7

The first balloon
ascent from
Vienna, 1784.

Souvenir
programme for
the Hendon air
show, 1910s.

FLYING
AT
HENDON

OFFICIAL
SOUVENIR
OF THE
LONDON AERODROME

in 1918. Despite these circumstances, the first commercial airline flying aircraft, Deutsche Luft Reederei (a forerunner of Lufthansa), was founded in 1917, although its services did not begin for another year.

In the United Kingdom civil flying was banned until May 1919. The potential for commercial aviation was recognised by many, though, and a Department of Civil Aviation was set up. In the immediate post-war years a number of air-travel companies were established in Europe, the United States and Australia. Their initial focus was on the transport of freight, especially mail,

Passengers and their pilot, Claude Grahame-White, on board the Grahame-White Type 10 Charabanc, Hendon, 1914.

Passengers waiting to board the Handley Page O/400 converted aircraft at Cricklewood aerodrome, north-west London, for their flight to Paris, c. 1919. Note the flying clothing worn by the pilot and several passengers.

but some passenger services were also offered. Flights were slow compared to the speeds of today, but the aeroplane was faster than travelling by rail or sea, and this appealed to many businessmen. In some countries, such as Australia, air travel offered the best means of getting from one place to another.

Aircraft Transport and Travel (AT&T), a subsidiary of the British manufacturing firm Airco, flew the first scheduled international passenger

flight in the summer of 1919. This took place between London (Hounslow Heath) and Paris (Le Bourget). AT&T was soon joined by other businesses, and services between Europe's leading capitals became available to those who could afford them. As air forces shrank after the war, many of the companies purchased surplus military aircraft and employed skilled pilots who had served in the war. These pilots had sole responsibility for their passengers and the aircraft. In addition to an annual salary, they received flying pay, calculated from a set amount for each hour in the air.

Conditions in these converted military aeroplanes were basic. Customers often had to climb or be helped into seats that were exposed to the elements. Some amenities were available, however, and Handley Page Transport offered the first post-war in-flight refreshments. These consisted of lunch baskets available for an extra 3s. For customers of AT&T the loan of flying clothing was included in their fare. In aircraft with enclosed cabins passengers sat on wicker chairs bolted to the floor. These were widely spaced out so that there was plenty of leg-room, but no seat-belts were available. A toilet was often provided, but it was rather primitive, and located behind a curtain.

To ensure the aircraft was not overloaded, passengers, as well as their luggage, were weighed in the 1920s.

These early flights could take longer than their advertised time as they were dependent on the weather and the well-being of the 'stick and string' aircraft. Unscheduled stops for refuelling or repairs often had to be made along the way. Operating companies were known to issue money to their pilots in case the aircraft could not be fixed. If this happened, passengers would then be given the money so that they could reach their destination by alternative means.

Such discomforts or inconveniences seem to have been happily endured by those being flown. They were offset by the sheer novelty and allure of travelling in an aircraft. Although expensive, flying was quick, modern and adventurous. It rapidly became a fashionable thing to do and a symbol of your status. The premier route took place between London and Paris.

During the 1920s numerous air-travel companies were formed in the rush to exploit this new technology and to earn a profit. The customer base at this time, however, remained comparatively small and, with the industry still finding its feet, many companies ran into difficulties and had to cease operating. Several European governments, including those of France and Germany, supported their air-travel businesses – but not the United Kingdom. As a result, British companies experienced a crisis in 1921, but government subsidies were forthcoming and enabled services to be resumed, with companies agreeing to apportion certain routes among themselves.

From the mid-1920s developments took place that enhanced the passenger experience. Companies were conscious of the level of comfort enjoyed by their wealthy clientele when travelling by train or ocean liner and so gave priority to the service provided to them. Customers could expect motor cars to take them to the airfield or to meet them on arrival. Pilots attended to all customs arrangements and, if all ran smoothly, passengers could expect to be in the air ten minutes after arriving at the airfield. This was probably just as well as facilities on the ground were minimal. If the weather delayed their flight, customers would have to wait in a cold wooden hut. By the end of the 1920s, however, buildings comparable to railway terminals were being built at European airports. Schiphol (Amsterdam), for example, had a hotel, café and restaurant available to its passengers. Croydon, which took over from Hounslow Heath as the London terminal airport in March 1920, was redeveloped and had stylish modern buildings by 1928.

New aircraft were built specifically for passenger travel and with comfort in mind. Among the first aircraft designed for civilians were the Handley Page W8A and the De Havilland DH18. Customers enjoyed well-ventilated cabins crafted from mahogany, fitted with upholstered armchairs, and featuring sliding glass windows that could be opened to improve the view. Despite restrictions placed on German production after the First World War, that country produced some outstanding civil aircraft in the 1920s. The Fokker VII was used by the Dutch

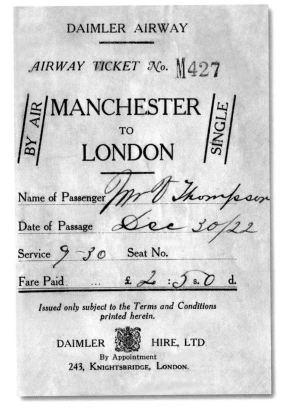

Daimler Airway ticket issued to Mr Thompson, 1922. The flight was undertaken by eight passengers on a De Havilland DH34.

airline Koninklijke Luchtvaart Maatschappij NV (KLM) and was equipped with radio telephony that enabled the crew to communicate with their colleagues on the ground. It also had a heated cabin furnished with chairs with sponge-rubber seating. Deutsche Lufthansa was formed in 1926 and used Junkers F.13 aircraft that had chairs fitted with seat-belts. The cockpit, for the first time, had dual controls, so that the physical effort of handling the aircraft could now be shared between a captain and his first officer. During this period pilots were also making the adjustment to flying within an enclosed cabin. Hitherto they were used to flying in open cockpits and felt that this provided them with better visibility. Nonetheless, the change was gradually accepted and was no doubt appreciated as the speed capability of aircraft increased.

With British companies continuing to struggle, the Hambling Committee recommended the formation of a new commercial organisation run along business lines, but which would receive government support. The national airline Imperial Airways Limited was created by merging Handley Page Transport, Instone Air Line Ltd, Daimler Airway and British Marine Air Navigation Company (BMAN). Operations were due to begin across Europe on 1 April 1924 but were delayed because of a strike by its pilots, who were concerned about pay and conditions. They agreed to a salary of £800 a year and flights began on 24 April 1924.

Imperial Airways worked hard to perpetuate the glamorous image of flying by advertising its clientele of royalty, film stars and famous personalities. Services were pitched at those who were in a position to enjoy them. There were no distinct 'classes' on board aircraft at this time, but a range of fares was offered on the company's flights to Europe's capitals, so that passengers could pay for what they required. A convenient flying time was available in a

The lavish interior of the Handley Page W8 featuring upholstered chairs and curtains at the windows.

new, comfortable, modern aircraft such as the Armstrong Whitworth Argosy, or a slower, cheaper flight could be taken at a less convenient time and in an older, more basic aircraft such as the Handley Page HP66. The first truly luxurious air service was introduced by Imperial Airways in 1927. Their 'Silver Wing' service to Paris was expensive and exclusive. On these flights the airline steward made his first ever appearance. Dressed in a smart white jacket, bow tie and cap, he served a first-class meal and drinks to the passengers. The pre-cooked food was heated up and presented on the finest of china upon small tables with linen cloths, silver cutlery and crystal glasses, a service comparable to that found in the high-class London restaurants of the period.

Today air travel is all about getting from A to B in the quickest time possible. In the 1920s flying was the fastest way to travel and, although speed fitted into the lifestyle of many 'bright young things' in the 'Roaring Twenties', it was not the priority for the majority of airline customers. It was the experience of flying which appealed – and the kudos achieved from doing so. The basic passenger service available at the beginning of the decade had improved considerably by its end, and yet the romance and comfort enjoyed by these early passengers would be taken to a new level during the 1930s.

Timetable for Imperial Airways' 'Silver Wing' service, 1927.

An Imperial Airways steward serving food to passengers.

Vol. CXLII. No. 1846.   THE BYSTANDER, M

The BYSTANDER

FLYING NUMBER 1/-

GLAMOUR AND COMFORT

IF THE 1920s witnessed the birth of commercial air travel, then the 1930s saw its coming of age: passengers were provided with a level of comfort unequalled since, and the extent of air routes available across oceans and continents appeared to shrink the world.

Commercial companies continued to promote this new form of transport as a viable alternative to the traditional ways of travelling for those who could afford it. The comfort and service enjoyed by their customers continued to be a priority, and inspiration was drawn from the ocean liners and trains of the period. New aircraft, such as the elegant and graceful Handley Page HP42, were designed and built with this in mind. Sheer luxury never before seen on an aircraft was a feature of their Pulman interiors. Proper wash-basins were fitted in the 'powder rooms', and the best woods and fabrics were used. Seating was researched extensively. Chairs were made that could be adjusted to any position, vertically or horizontally. Those on the HP42 were the lightest and most comfortable lounge chairs constructed. Call buttons, reading lights and folding tables were incorporated, and passengers were assured of being well looked after by the cabin staff. Stewards offered a silver service, and passengers could enjoy meals of several courses. Dining was a sophisticated procedure, with tables dressed with linen, while silver cutlery and the best crystal were used. A number of companies had bone-china tea sets made that featured their logo. Customers no longer had to board via a ladder but used a few shallow steps, sometimes with a covered walkway attached to them.

Cabin staff had been introduced during the 1920s, but until the 1930s all new recruits were male. During that decade the first female stewardesses were employed by the American company Boeing Air Transport, later to be a part of United Airlines. Ellen Church, a registered nurse from Iowa, initially applied to the company to be a pilot but was turned down. However, she did convince the company of the psychological advantage in having women on board flights. She argued that this would have a calming effect on those customers fearful of flying. There was also the added 'care factor' in that

Opposite:
The *Bystander* magazine produced specific 'Flying Number' issues dedicated to promoting air travel. This colourful, graphic front cover design by Lowen from 1939 features a flying boat landing near an exotic Mediterranean location.

Interior view of the passenger cabin of the Handley Page HP42, known as the 'Winged Cunarder' because of the level of comfort, comparable to ocean liners of the day.

Passengers disembarking at night from a four-engined Armstrong Whitworth AW27 Ensign.

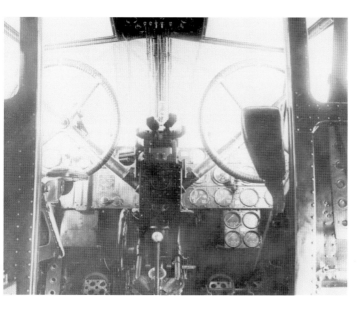

View of a Handley
Page HP42 cockpit.
Note the huge
steering-wheel
controls used
by the crew
to manoeuvre
the aircraft.

the stewardesses were there specifically to look after the passengers. The
first stewardesses were registered nurses, and for many years a nursing
qualification was a key requirement in the recruitment of stewardesses.

Despite the attention to and focus on the passenger's experience, this
was still affected by the technological limitations of the day. Aircraft were
now made of metal, and therefore more robust than their wooden
predecessors. Consequently, they were more reliable and offered a greater
degree of service regularity, but they were still noisy. Customers were
issued with earplugs to help counter this. Some soundproofing was also
attempted, with special bulkheads fitted, and the positioning of seats
was considered in relation to the
vibration felt from the engines.
Specially thickened window glass
could also be found on some
aircraft. Safety continued to be a
prime concern, particularly after
a number of crashes took place
in the early 1930s. The airlines
did their best to reassure their
customers. Imperial Airways had a
policy of using aircraft with four
engines for this purpose, and they
stressed this in their advertising.

Information card
issued to
passengers letting
them know the
arrangements for
a particular day
during the journey.
Details include
timings and the
name of the
Imperial Airways
representative at
the station at Juba
in Sudan.

IMPERIAL AIRWAYS
JUBA

Station		
ARRANGEMENTS FOR	10/8/35	
You will be called at	0545	and your baggage should be outside
your room at	0615	
Breakfast	will be served	0615
Currency Coupons will be cashed at	P. 24	
The car will leave	0645	at
The air-liner will leave the airport at	0700	hours to-morrow and stops
will be made at	Malakal and Khartoum	

Meals on to-morrow's journey will be served as shown.

BREAKFAST	Juba	TEA	Khartoum
LUNCH	in flight	DINNER	Khartoum

Mr. Adams the Company's representative, will give to you
any further information or assistance you may need during your stay at this station

With an eye on profitability, the airlines chose to invest in larger aircraft during this period. As a consequence the passenger experience became more 'communal', with numbers increasing from four to six customers on board to between eighteen and twenty, and even rising to forty before the decade was over. There was still plenty of space, however, with passengers having the opportunity to move from their seat to a viewing point or to use a lounge during the journey. Operating on such a scale and incorporating new technological features had an impact on the crews too. Enclosed cockpits became standard and were much more spacious than earlier ones had been. They were almost all fitted with dual controls, and the captain was joined by a first officer and a radio operator. Following pioneering work by the Germans in the 1920s, training in instrument flying became available, and short-haul night flights were offered to the public on some routes for the first time. Until then, all flights had been flown during the day. During the 1930s services continued to stop during the winter and there was no flying on Sundays or bank holidays.

The German Graf Zeppelin LZ 127 shown on a poster advertising the route to South America in 1935.

During this period airlines flew longer distances than ever before. KLM had pioneered long-haul flights in 1925, providing a 9,500-mile service to the Dutch East Indies, and this route was now joined by many others across the world. Sir Alan Cobham had undertaken pioneering survey flights in the 1920s for Imperial Airways. As a result of these, the company, with the help of partners such as Qantas, had established the foundations of their route network by the mid-1930s, providing links between most parts of the British Empire and a number of other countries. These flights had the effect of making the world seem smaller for the first time, but they were a considerable undertaking, with some equating to what today would be an exclusive tour of

several weeks. The Imperial Airways service from the United Kingdom to South Africa, available from 1932, could take eleven days and incorporated twenty-eight stops, two railway connections and five different types of aircraft. The trip to Australia took twelve days; this is a long time by today's standard but it was thirty days shorter than making the journey by ship. Following transoceanic survey flights by Charles Lindbergh for Pan Am, the airline started its scheduled service from San Francisco to Hong Kong in 1936, using Glen Martin 130 flying boats. This 4,000-mile journey took just three days, compared to the three-week journey by ship, for a return fare equal to the average American annual wage. The exclusive comfort available on these long-distance flights and their image of romance and adventure are epitomised by the airship and the flying boat.

Until the *Hindenburg* disaster of 1937, airships were seen as a luxurious way to travel and the best option for long-distance flying by air. They could fly for about forty hours before needing to be refuelled, and in the 1920s, unlike most contemporary aircraft, their capacity enabled them to fly across oceans. Most European countries experimented with airships until crashes, such as that of the R101 in 1928, put a stop to further trials. Germany, however, persevered and launched the Graf Zeppelin in September 1928. The size of four modern jumbo jets, it flew twenty passengers on a worldwide trip. With the airship moored close to the ground, the passengers and crew could board by climbing a short flight of steps built into the gondola. Full kitchen facilities, a dining room and bedrooms with windows were available. Between 1936 and 1937 the *Hindenburg* undertook ten trips across the Atlantic. Passengers enjoyed a very comfortable, warm and quiet journey. The main compartments, such as the dining room and lounge, were large and spacious; styled by Professor Fritz Breuhaus, they had a clean, modern look. The tables and chairs were made from lightweight tubular aluminium, and the walls were decorated with silk wallpaper. With luxurious facilities comparable to those found on board contemporary ocean liners, travelling by airship was a majestic way to fly, the like of which has not been experienced since.

The colossal airship sheds at Cardington, Bedfordshire, which housed the R101.

Flying boats were another wonder of the age. They were a prestigious form of transport that featured in the movies of the time. An awe-inspiring sight, these large and spacious aircraft gracefully took off and landed on water, offering a first-class service for no more than forty passengers at a time. For the first time two decks were incorporated into aircraft design. On the Short S.23 Empire Class flying boat, for example, the crew, mail and luggage occupied the top 'flight deck' while the passengers were seated on the lower deck, where they could enjoy a library, a smoking room and a promenade area. There was also a fully equipped kitchen and

A passenger cabin on the Graf Zeppelin LZ 127, showing the sleeping accommodation. The cabin's window is visible on the far wall.

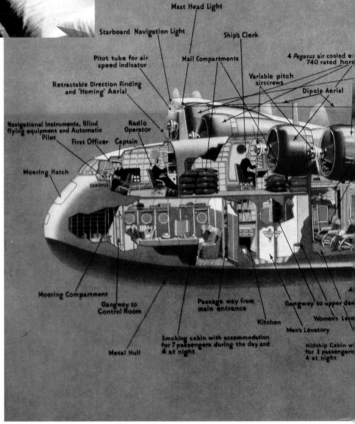

Mast Head Light

Starboard Navigation Light

Ship's Clerk

Pitot tube for air speed indicator

Mail Compartments

4 *Pegasus* air cooled e 740 rated hor

Retractable Direction Finding and 'Homing' Aerial

Variable pitch airscrews

Dipole Aerial

Navigational Instruments, Blind flying equipment and Automatic Pilot

Radio Operator

First Officer Captain

Mooring Hatch

CANOPUS

Mooring Compartment

Gangway to Control Room

Passage way from main entrance

Gangway to upper de

Kitchen

Women's Lava

Men's Lavatory

Smoking cabin with accommodation for 7 passengers during the day and 4 at night

Metal Hull

Midship Cabin w for 3 passenger 4 at night

well-stocked bar. Imperial Airways used a variety of flying boats over the years on their Empire routes to places such as South Africa. Because flying boats were able to make use of lakes, seas and oceans located along the routes, it was felt that this form of aircraft was a cheaper option than building new airstrips on land. They were also seen as safer in this respect than land-planes as their routes tended to take them over large amounts of water. They would have the option to come down safely if difficulties arose. Because they flew in warmer, more humid climates, leather padded seats and wood were used instead of fabric on board. Sleeping berths were available on some flying boats, but generally long-distance flights were completed in stages during the daytime. At stops along the way the passengers disembarked via motor launches and were conveyed to first-class accommodation provided nearby. The fares for these journeys continued to be very expensive but did include

Fixed aerial

Freight hatch here

al wing

International Registration Marking

Hold for bedding

NHI

Mail, Freight and Baggage hold

Port navigation light

Flaps fitted to trailing edges of the wing

After cabin with accommodation for 6 passengers during the day and 4 at night

Wing tip float

gangway

Promenade cabin with accommodation for 8 passengers during the day and 4 at night

The Imperial Airways flying boat *Canopus*, a popular passenger carrier of the 1930s. Cutaway diagram published in 1936.

21

A vintage Dragon
Rapide in flight.

the cost of the additional transport, food and lodging that were a feature of the journey.

As in the 1920s, there were different types of flights available in the United Kingdom for different clientele. Various joy-rides existed. The cost of an Imperial Airways afternoon-tea flight over London, for example, was the same as an average working man's weekly wage. For a couple of pounds customers could move about in the cabin, enjoy the novelty of viewing sights such as the Houses of Parliament from the air, and be served an afternoon tea in sumptuous comfort. Other companies, such as Sir Alan Cobham's Flying Circus, offered a short flight of several minutes. Thousands paid the few shillings 'to be up to date and aviate'. In an extension of this joy-riding idea, and by using small modern aircraft such as the De Havilland Dragon Rapide DH89, domestic regional services at reasonable prices were provided by a number of different airlines. These proved to be very popular, and a network of airports was built during this period, with Speke (Liverpool), Ringway (Manchester), Gatwick and Luton among those established. The government became concerned by the burgeoning number of airlines and encouraged them to merge to survive. It sought some control over the air-travel industry and appointed the Maybury Committee to advise it on a planned system for the country. The committee's report in 1936

Advertising leaflets
for independent
airways operating
in the United
Kingdom during
the 1930s.

recommended the licensing of a single company to link Great Britain's main cities. This situation had, however, already been effectively achieved although some companies, such as Channel Island Airways and several in the Scottish Highlands, remained independent. In 1934 the Railway Air Services (RAS) had been formed and in co-operation with other companies was working towards providing customers with a coherent pattern of domestic routes. In 1935 Spartan Airlines, Hillman Airways and United Airways merged to form British Airways (BA). In light of the services being provided by RAS, BA decided to focus on European routes not flown by Imperial Airways.

When the Prime Minister, Neville Chamberlain, flew to Munich in 1938 to speak with the German Chancellor, Adolf Hitler, after German troops entered Czechoslovakia, he did so in a British Airways aircraft. In front of the modern and stylish Lockheed Electra, he famously stated that there 'would be peace in our time'. Regrettably, he was proved wrong the following year when Germany invaded Poland. On 3 September 1939 Great Britain declared war on Germany and the Second World War began. In a reversal of events at the end of the First World War, when surplus military aircraft had been used for commercial purposes, civil aircraft were made available for the war effort. The ultimate glamour, luxury and style of flying in the 1930s came to an end and a new era in air travel began.

The Prime Minister, Neville Chamberlain, at Heston Airport in front of a Lockheed Electra after returning from Munich. He holds the piece of paper signed by the German Chancellor, Adolf Hitler, and himself, 3 October 1938.

THE WAR YEARS

THE SECOND WORLD WAR had a huge impact on air travel. The services available to passengers were severely affected, and those working for the airlines did so under dangerous conditions. The technological advances in aircraft manufacturing made during the war were incorporated into new commercial designs that became available in the post-war years.

Under wartime conditions, seats on passenger flights were hard to come by. Priority was given to serving personnel, government officials, VIPs, and those whose trips were vital to the war effort. Members of the public able to buy tickets experienced disruption, diversions and delays. They also had to be ready to depart at very short notice. Increased security procedures added time to the journey, and black-out measures on the aircraft windows blocked any views. Passengers were conscious of the inherent dangers of flying but they also became aware of the added peril during wartime. A number of commercial aircraft were lost through enemy action, including a Douglas DC-3 that was shot down on 1 June 1943 while on a flight to Lisbon. The actor Leslie Howard was among those on board who were killed. For those lucky enough to obtain seats on flights out of enemy-occupied territories such as the Channel Islands, travelling by air was a lifeline, and a couple of hours of risk was a small price to pay for freedom.

Commercial airline companies such as British Overseas Aircraft Corporation (BOAC), which had been formed in 1939 with the merger of Imperial Airways and British Airways, worked hard to keep their services running for as long as possible. As the war progressed, however, disruption and the closure of many routes took place. As Germany now controlled most of Europe, only Lufthansa operated fully in this region. Neutral airports such as Lisbon were in use for a few years, enabling other companies to offer limited flights. Italy's entry into the war effectively closed the Mediterranean to British commercial flying, and, as Japanese forces advanced through the Far East, the long-haul routes flown through this region were suspended. Some journeys, however, continued to be possible. American companies undertook flights across the Atlantic, finishing at the neutral airport of Foynes in Ireland. Flights via the Azores and Bermuda were also available. The British Prime Minister, Sir Winston Churchill, flew as a passenger on BOAC aircraft several times during 1942 between the United Kingdom and the United States. He was conscious of the advantage provided to him in being able to make the journey in eighteen hours.

Many companies focused their resources on contributing to the war effort, and their work was vital to the Allied cause. Air France, for example, which had the third largest route network in 1939, operated elements of this to support the Free French forces. BOAC meanwhile maintained its 'Horseshoe' route from Durban to Sydney via Cairo and Karachi for as long as it could. Communications between London and Cairo, for instance, were kept open because of the flights flown by BOAC crews. Wing Officer Hayes

A Douglas Dakota of BOAC, silhouetted at night by the batteries of searchlights at Gibraltar, as it is prepared for a flight to the United Kingdom.

Women pilots of
the Air Transport
Auxiliary (ATA)
standing next to an
Airspeed Oxford:
(left to right)
Lettice Curtis,
Jenny Broad,
Audrey Sale-
Barker, Gabrielle
Patterson,
Pauline Gower.

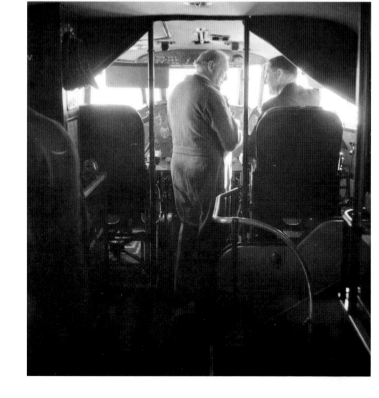

The Prime
Minister, Winston
Churchill, talks
to a member of
the crew in the
cockpit of the
Boeing 314 flying
boat *Berwick* in
January 1942
during his
journey from
Bermuda back
to Great Britain.

was sent out to the Middle East in 1942 to investigate the possibility of setting up a Women's Auxiliary Air Force (WAAF) contingent in this theatre. In her report she praised the 'careful' flying 'of the BOAC pilots and kindly consideration of the other members of the crews' during her daunting 3,600-mile journey. Flying unarmed, these men were often to be found within battle zones dropping supplies or evacuating troops. In the United Kingdom, the Air Transport Auxiliary (ATA), run by BOAC, consisted of 1,245 civilian male and female pilots from twenty-five different countries. They ferried over 300,000 aircraft for the Royal Air Force (RAF) and Royal Navy between the factories and the various airfields where they were most needed.

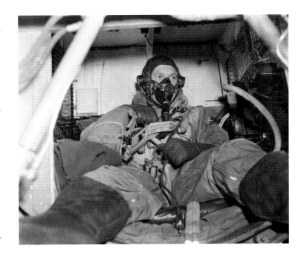

A passenger travelling in the bomb bay of a De Havilland Mosquito of BOAC, on the fast freight service between Leuchars, Fife, and Stockholm, Sweden.

Important pioneering work was also undertaken during the war years. Several highly skilled BOAC crews, including the Australian Captain Donald Bennett, who would later command the RAF Pathfinder Force, developed the North Atlantic Air Route. This established for the first time an all-year-round, two-way service for land-planes between the United Kingdom and Canada. This route was essential in enabling American-built aircraft to be flown to Great Britain, boosting the resources of the RAF immensely.

Necessity also inspired ingenuity. Flights to and from Stockholm were vitally important in maintaining the critical supply of ball-bearings to Britain's manufacturing industry. Crews ferried officials involved in this process, and the vital ball-bearings. The fast night fighter De Havilland Mosquito aircraft was later used for this work. There was no room for passengers in the cabin, and so it was decided to line the bomb bays with felt and fit them with seat-belts. The passenger, wrapped up in flying clothing, would be strapped in and given some sandwiches and a flask of coffee for the journey. An electric light was rigged up so that he could read and an intercom allowed him to speak with the pilot.

Civilian crews showed huge dedication and courage in undertaking this work, with some paying the ultimate sacrifice and losing their lives. After the Second World War had finished, Sir Winston Churchill expressed his opinion on the important contribution made by the civilian airlines and their employees. He wrote that 'Victory is the beautiful bright-coloured flower … transport is the stem without which it could never have blossomed'.

A civil-registered Avro Tudor C5, G-AKBZ *Star Falcon*, of British South American Airways, at Wunstorf aerodrome during the Berlin Airlift, 1948.

When the conflict was over, commercial services were reinstated. In the United Kingdom plans were made for services to be provided by three state corporations. BOAC continued to operate the long-haul flights to the Empire, Far East and North America. British European Airways (BEA) took over the European and domestic services. British South American Airways (BSAA) operated between the United Kingdom and South American destinations, as well as the Caribbean. Various aircraft were available for these routes. BOAC refurbished the flying boats, which had been in service with the RAF, and the pre-war way of flying resumed for a short time. The appeal of this form of air travel was strong after the dark days of conflict. The flights also offered a unique experience for passengers. Air traffic control was not as strict as it is today and Flight Lieutenant Eric Woods, serving as navigator on the flying-boat route to South Africa, recalls that his captain would take slight detours from the flight plan. He would drop several hundred feet to show his passengers the wildlife on the African Savannah. BOAC pilots also had a tradition of banking their aircraft when passing over the Victoria Falls to allow the passengers a good view of this natural spectacle. The personal relationship between the crew and their customers was still strong. The officers would take it in turns to walk around the main cabin, talking to passengers, pointing out landmarks and answering questions. On the long-haul flights both crew and passengers would stay overnight at the same 'rest house' along the route and socialise. However, the 'slip' system worked by airlines such as BOAC did limit a passenger's time with one crew. The whole flight may have taken place in the one aircraft but different crews flew different stages.

In parallel to this traditional way of flying, new aircraft that changed the passenger experience appeared during the post-war years. Civil versions of military aircraft that had been used during the war, for example the Avro Lancastrian, Avro York and Avro Tudor, were employed. They went faster than anything previously flown and travelled twice as far without the need to be refuelled. The Boeing 307 Stratoliner was the first pressurised aircraft, and the Lockheed Constellation was the first pressurised transatlantic airliner, enabling passengers to be flown over, rather than through, bad weather. They also offered a high level of comfort and speed.

These new aircraft were larger and heavier than older models and required concrete runways rather than the traditional soft earth. In consequence, airports had to raise their standards and needed to expand. In the United Kingdom the main land-plane terminal had relocated for the duration of the war but the authorities came to realise that it needed to be closer to London. Croydon was too small, and encroaching suburbia prevented expansion. Heathrow was identified as an alternative. It had been used during the war by the RAF and so it had concrete runways, but as yet no terminal buildings. Marquees and caravans were used as an intermediate measure as the site became established as 'London Airport'. When it opened on 31 May 1946, long-haul flights operated by BOAC and BSAA were available. Over the next few decades Heathrow, its amenities and the flights it provided expanded greatly in an attempt to keep pace with the increasing numbers of passengers travelling by air.

Following spread: Heathrow Airport seen from the air in 1956. Development is clearly under way but the site has a long way to go to reach its current scale of operation.

Captain Alan Bray DFC speaking with passengers in-flight between Khartoum and Nairobi, 1948.

29

Comet Jetliner

Stratocruiser

Hermes

Constellation

Argonaut

B·O·A·C *takes good care of you*

THE B.O.A.C. FLEET comprises five of the finest types of civil aircraft—Comet Jetliner, Stratocruiser, Hermes, Constellation and Argonaut—all four-engined, air-conditioned and pressurized for smooth above-the-weather flying. Each offers all the refinements of modern luxury air travel; spacious cabins; supremely comfortable, adjustable chairs; tasteful decor in soft pastel shades; good, yet restful lighting; roomy, fully-equipped dressing rooms. The B.O.A.C. Comet, the first pure jet airliner to fly on civil air routes, combines speed with graceful elegance. At eight miles a minute, flying times are almost halved on the routes it serves. The Hermes, Constellation and Argonaut are, of course, established favourites. Each has special passenger features known and enjoyed by those who fly by B.O.A.C. The Stratocruiser has full-length sleepers available for a small extra charge and this double-decked airliner has a luxurious cocktail lounge on the lower deck, where passengers may enjoy the gay atmosphere of transatlantic air travel at its best.

In flight, ever-attentive stewards and a stewardess anticipate your every wish. You are served with delicious complimentary meals, including meal-time drinks, and with light refreshments at any time. A wide variety of passenger amenities is provided for your entertainment and a well-stocked bar at duty free prices is always carried. Throughout your journey by B.O.A.C. you are given the finest service—efficient, courteous, and friendly.

HIGHER, FURTHER, FASTER

THE 1950s was a decade of innovation for air travel. As well as developments within the airline industry, new types of aeroplane entered commercial service. In particular the introduction of jet aircraft heralded a new era, with passengers able to travel faster than ever before.

By 1950, airline passengers had been travelling in propeller-driven piston-engine aircraft for several decades and continued to do so. Technical advances had continuously increased the capabilities of these aeroplanes. Recent developments in aircraft design as a result of the Second World War were being adopted in commercial aviation. Pressurisation was the latest innovation to be introduced: in effect, an internal atmosphere was created on board an aircraft, so that it could fly higher than ever before, for example at 20,000 feet, while its occupants effectively flew at a 'lower' altitude, for example 3,000 feet, because the cabin's air pressure was maintained at a constant breathable level. The difference was noticeable when coming into land, however, and airlines offered barley sugars to their customers to suck in an attempt to offset the pressure built up on their ears during landing. This was a feature on many new aircraft such as the Boeing Stratocruiser, Lockheed Constellation and Douglas DC-6. The Handley Page Hermes and Canadair version of the Douglas DC-4, employed by BOAC as its Argonaut class, replaced the older flying boats on the Commonwealth routes. These aircraft were very popular with passengers because they were able to fly over turbulence caused by bad weather rather than having to go through it.

Many passengers in the 1950s were able to fly to their holiday destination in a turbo-prop aircraft. The evolution of this engine design (which involved energy in a gas jet turning a turbine that turned the propeller) provided airline passengers with a quicker and quieter journey than that experienced in a piston-engine aircraft. The Vickers Viscount was the first turbo-prop aircraft to carry passengers on a scheduled service, in 1953 from London to Cyprus. This elegant, pioneering aircraft, which featured large panoramic windows, could carry forty-seven passengers, and by 1957 later versions could carry over fifty-seven. The Bristol Britannia, which came into service

Opposite: 'BOAC takes good care of you': an advertising leaflet showing customers the aircraft it operated as well as the attentive service they could expect during their flight.

Passengers
boarding a
Lockheed
Constellation.

Opposite:
An artistic poster
showing an
American city and
advertising that
the opportunity
to visit the United
States was
available to
passengers flying
with BOAC.

from 1955, was nicknamed the 'Whispering Giant' because of its size and because it generated much less noise than some of its contemporaries. The engines caused less vibration too, so passengers could also enjoy a much smoother, more comfortable flight.

In the 1950s passengers occupied spacious cabins that continued to resemble train carriages of the period in their layout. Seats were four abreast, two each side of the aisle, with some arranged in fours around a table. In their advertising the airlines stressed the pleasant atmosphere and the tastefully decorated cabins equipped with all the modern amenities. Luxury services were available, for example on board BOAC's 'Monarch' service between London and New York. This service initially used Boeing Stratocruisers, which offered sleeping accommodation and also featured sumptuous lounges fitted with well-stocked bars on the lower deck. Superb cuisine continued to be provided, and cabin staff brought the food to the customers on a trolley. They discussed the choices available and served the meals on plates in front of them. Technical developments and innovations in industry had an impact on air travel at this time. Plastic cutlery made its first appearance, replacing

A Handley Page
Hermes, 1950s.

the fine china previously used. On some flights frozen meals were introduced, although these were slow to catch on.

The 1950s was a decade of prosperity, with many more travellers making journeys by air. As in the past, people flew for different reasons. Travelling by air was, and continues to be, financially worthwhile for businessmen. For many people it continued to have a mystique and allure as well as prestige. The rich and powerful remained the major customers although the

Crew members
were also
served food
during the flight.

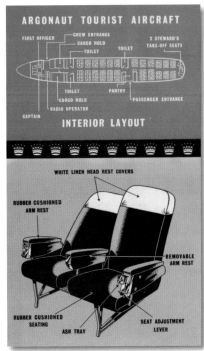

introduction of different 'class' fares during the 1950s provided the opportunity for a broader range of people to fly. The world's first 'tourist' fare (later to become 'economy class') was made available by BOAC on its North Atlantic route in 1952, and the first flights with mixed classes on board (first and tourist class) flew in 1958. The charter market also began at this time, and companies such as Dan Air transported considerable numbers of people during the winter months to destinations such as the Canary Islands. The opportunity to go somewhere different, to see new, exotic and colourful places, was a huge attraction – an out-of-the-ordinary and special experience. The airlines were conscious of this and their awareness is reflected in the advertising of the period. One could argue that they worked to instil

Above left:
Stewardesses
of BEA, 1950s.

Above:
Advertisement
highlighting the
layout of the
Argonaut Tourist
aircraft and the
comfortable chairs
on board.

Left: Colourful
BOAC leaflet
advertising flights
to East Africa,
1950s.

FLY to the
CHANNEL ISLANDS

FOR YOUR 1953 SUMMER HOLIDAY

BEA

BRITISH EUROPEAN AIRWAYS

BEA timetable
for services to the
Channel Islands,
a popular holiday
destination, 1953.

this image in the mind of the public. For the first time more people travelled across the Atlantic by air than by sea in 1957. Lufthansa, which had resumed its services in 1955, using Frankfurt as its base instead of Berlin, reported carrying 74,000 people in its first year. By 1959 this had grown to 786,000. The overall increase in passengers enabled many airlines to make a profit for the first time.

The move towards mass travel, which would come to dominate the next twenty years, is considered to have begun in the 1950s. Air travel in these years, however, retained a certain character. Passengers still wore their best clothes to fly, and it was still an exclusive activity that many saved up for. For the airlines, despite the push for faster, more frequent flights, a high level of service and attention given to their customers was considered essential. It was unthinkable at this time that passengers on the long-haul flights, such as those between London and Singapore, should arrive at their destinations fatigued or 'jet-lagged'.

In one major respect air travel was revolutionised during the 1950s. The first commercial jet, the British De Havilland Comet, flew passengers from London to Johannesburg (with stops) on 2 May 1952. Travelling at speeds of 450 mph, it offered the fastest journeys to date. The Comet had no precedent and was a huge leap forward compared to what had gone before. Unfortunately this sleek, modern aircraft, which offered its customers very comfortable surroundings, encountered difficulties, and a series of

Although its
heyday had been
during the 1930s,
the Ju52 continued
to be used by
some airlines in
the 1950s. This is a
view of its cockpit.

devastating crashes took place. The rest of the fleet was grounded, and the company spent a number of years analysing the crashes and redesigning the aircraft. It was discovered that the pressures placed on the airframe were too strong and the aircraft's structural integrity was compromised. For several years the only jet aircraft offering commercial flights was the Russian Tupolov Tu-104.

A BOAC De Havilland Comet jet airliner, en route to Johannesburg from London, breaking its journey at Entebbe Airport, Uganda.

After this stuttering start of a new era, further jet aircraft entered commercial service. In 1958 De Havilland launched its new improved version, the Comet 4, which undertook the first transatlantic crossing by a jet aircraft a few weeks before Pan Am flew its Boeing 707 on this route. This latter design could accommodate twice as many passengers as carried by the Comet and was faster, flying at 600 mph. Both of these aircraft were designed for long-haul flights where their speed cut down journey times dramatically, and, in terms of running costs, they proved efficient and reliable. Other companies focused on smaller aircraft for short to medium distances. The Sud Caravelle, for example, entered service with Air France in 1959. This stylish aircraft was the first to feature rear-mounted engines, which contributed to quieter journeys for customers. Flying on a jet proved extremely popular and created real excitement. If the development of flying can be equated with the innovation of computers, then jet airliners can be compared with the emergence of the laptop. The transition did not happen quickly but during the 1960s commercial passenger jets became firmly established.

THE JET AGE

D URING THE 1960s millions of ordinary people had the opportunity to
experience air travel and to fly in a jet aircraft for the first time. While
pressurised jet aircraft, such as the De Havilland Comet 4B and Boeing 707,
were in service during this period, older aircraft were still employed on some
routes. By the mid-1960s a new generation of jets was introduced. They
included the Hawker Siddeley Trident and the British Aircraft Corporation
BAC 111. The Vickers VC10, which entered service in 1964, was loved by
pilots because of its flying characteristics, and was popular with passengers
because its tail-mounted engines offered an even quieter journey.

The airlines had shared the excitement shown by the public about jet
aircraft. Initially this led to an over-capacity on some routes, with many
jets flying with empty seats. This situation was short-lived, however, as the
number of passengers on scheduled flights more than doubled during
the decade. By using this form of aeroplane on the majority of routes, airlines
incurred reduced running costs because the engines were more reliable,
faster and less expensive to run and maintain than the older piston engines.
As a consequence fares generally came down. This, combined with a wider
availability of economy class, led to increasing numbers of people being able
to fly outside their own country and see the wider world. Indeed, flying
had never been so popular. By 1960 BEA had carried its 25 millionth
passenger, and during March 1969 alone it carried 575,000 passengers. This
was fifteen thousand more people than the entire number of passengers
carried by Imperial Airways during its history between 1924 and 1938.

Flying continued to be an aspirational activity, and something of an
adventure. Its glamorous image was reinforced during the 1960s, when
the national newspapers were full of photographs showing film and pop
stars and other celebrities arriving or leaving by aeroplane. Articles
highlighted the rich and beautiful jetting around the world for pleasure.
In keeping with the 'Swinging Sixties' era, the image of the air stewardess
also underwent a change. Her uniform became colourful and stylish,
created for the airlines by leading fashion designers. The stewardess came

A passenger being served a first-class meal on board a BOAC De Havilland Comet jet aircraft, 1960s.

to epitomise female perfection and sex appeal, representing an exciting and glamorous way of life. Girls everywhere wanted to work for the airlines. During recruitment, emphasis was placed on youth and appearance, with strict age limits imposed. Applicants had to supply a photograph and

Members of the public viewing the Vickers Viscount aircraft parked on the tarmac next to a terminal building at Heathrow, 1960s.

Entries from Captain Bray's logbook recording the various destinations he flew to during 1963.

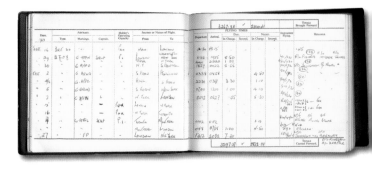

personal measurements. Interviews included a parade intended to show the panel a candidate's poise and deportment. The 'trolley dolly' image was popular but masked the fact that most of these women were intelligent, professional and exceptionally good at their job.

Although the aircraft were becoming larger, the number of passengers accommodated on board remained within the range of one or two hundred. This enabled the stewardesses to maintain a high level of personal attention to each customer. They had the time to engage and talk with them as well as serving refreshments and looking after them. This relationship was stressed by the airlines, rather than the traditional one between the passengers and their pilot. Previously the captain would leave the cockpit during the flight and chat with his passengers, but this was gradually phased out during the 1960s. With the introduction of intercoms and radio announcements, the relationship became quite distant. Some traditions continued, however, with flight information being passed from the cockpit around the cabin on a card, and, where appropriate, a Crossing the Equator certificate was issued to passengers.

Jet travel offered customers greater speed and a smoother journey, although it was found that flying at speeds of over 500 mph and at higher altitudes had an effect upon the human body. People had an inability to cope with the swiftly

Air France advertisement featuring an air hostess, 1966.

changing time zones and this led to the phrase 'jet-lag', and human physiology was altered by spending time in a cabin kept at a lower pressure to that outside. Feet and ankles became swollen and skin reacted to the drier air. These disadvantages do not appear to have deterred customers, and passengers continued to take pleasure in this modern way of travel. On board they could enjoy the comfort provided in the cabins. Experts designed restful interiors, resulting in the walls and ceilings being painted in soft greys, beiges and blues, while pastels were employed for chairs and pillows.

In-flight entertainment had traditionally consisted of the facilities available to passengers such as separate lounges and promenade decks, as well as the services provided by the cabin staff. Smoking was still permitted on board. The food and drink served during a flight had progressed from coffee and sandwiches at an extra cost to complimentary meals served in a dining cabin or to the individual in his or her seat. In the 1960s the current way of eating on an aeroplane was introduced. Free pre-cooked meals heated up in-flight were served to the passenger on fold-down trays in front of

The Beatles return from Paris on a BEA flight, landing at Heathrow Airport, 1964. They are holding BEA-branded bags.

British Aircraft
Corporation cabin
interior, mid-
1960s.

BEA menu card
informing
passengers about
the food available
to them in-flight.

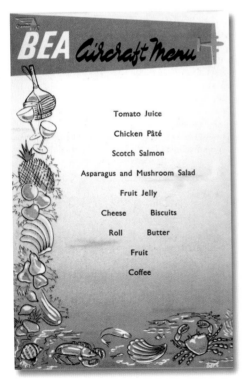

BEA *Aircraft Menu*

Tomato Juice

Chicken Pâté

Scotch Salmon

Asparagus and Mushroom Salad

Fruit Jelly

Cheese   Biscuits

Roll   Butter

Fruit

Coffee

their seat. The airline companies employed top designers to create suitable tableware and trays for this purpose. Acclaimed chefs produced the menus for them. Films also became a regular feature on long-haul journeys during this period. These proved very popular, and passengers enjoyed the novelty of having a single movie showing on a central screen for the whole cabin.

With the different airlines using similar aircraft, offering standardised fares and regulated food and drink, one might think that there was not much difference between them by this time. The companies themselves were conscious of this and emphasised their individual identities. Air India, for example, advertised that they would make 'passengers feel like maharajahs'. Its stewardesses wore traditional Indian dress, while the aircraft were decorated appropriately. Many airlines handed out complimentary branded gifts to passengers, including packs of playing cards, toys, items of stationery and luggage.

Other innovations took place during the 1960s. The way in which airports were managed developed, with changes implemented to cater for the larger aircraft and greater numbers passing through. Previously, passengers had walked out to the aircraft on the grass or tarmac and climbed a set of movable stairs, or later 'air stairs' built into the aircraft. Now, 'jet bridges' were used extensively around the world. The jet bridge in use today is an enclosed, movable walkway linking the terminal gate to the aircraft's doorway.

Runways were extended and new methods for baggage handling were introduced. The air traffic control systems were also updated, and BEA became the first airline outside the United States to employ a fully automated system for booking seats. Despite these efforts, large numbers of people experienced long delays awaiting their flights at the airport, and these became a regular occurence during the 1970s.

Above and below: In the 1960s a printed flight guide was presented to passengers so they could see the planned route for their journey.

THE BOOM IN AIR TRAVEL

THE 1970s was the start of the age of the jumbo jet and mass travel. It was also the decade in which supersonic flight became a feature of commercial passenger travel.

Many airlines continued to use the aircraft they had flown in the 1960s, for example the Hawker Siddeley Trident, with the latest versions entering service during the new decade. New jet aircraft such as the Douglas DC-10, Lockheed Tristar and Airbus 300 provided customers with comfortable, fast flights over short to medium distances, and new turbo-prop aircraft such as the Hawker Siddeley HS748 were also used on regional and domestic routes. In the 1970s the airline industry embraced the Boeing 747 and operated it on long-haul journeys. The aircraft is an icon of this period and represents the modern era of passenger travel. It has spawned many different series or 'generations', and the latest continues to fly today. The jumbo jet was huge, the largest commercial aircraft to fly at that time. Its length was greater than the distance first flown by the Wright Brothers in 1903, and the height from the ground to the top of its tail was equivalent to a six-floor building. By the end of its first year one hundred 747s were flying commercially and had carried seven million passengers. In its first three years of service thirty-five million customers had flown on this type of aircraft.

With a nod to the past, its internal layout initially allowed room for lounges with pianos and bars as a way of encouraging passengers to fly. These quickly disappeared, however, to be replaced with more seating. The jumbo jet's prime objective was to carry as many passengers as it could to its various destinations. The first of the wide-bodied aircraft, the Boeing 747, accommodated over four hundred people in first or economy class. For the first time cabins featured two aisles, and rows of ten seats. For passengers in economy class this meant a loss of space and less personal attention from the cabin staff. Given the size of the cabins, different groups of stewards and stewardesses looked after specific 'sections'. Former employees of the airlines have commented that their working conditions changed during the 1970s. The camaraderie enjoyed by the smaller numbers of staff on board an aircraft

Opposite:
The head of Laker Airways, Freddie Laker, mingles with passengers on board his transatlantic Skytrain flight from London to New York, 17 June 1979.

47

An El Al Boeing 747 taking off over rooftops near Heathrow Airport in 1971.

British Airways stewardesses show off a classic and elegant new uniform designed by the British fashion house Baccarat. The new uniforms were in service by 1978.

in earlier periods was lost as each group formed its own unit. There was an increase in workload too, with the number of passengers requiring attention having risen, and their working hours becoming longer, with journeys having fewer stop-overs. Pilots who flew the Boeing 747 have stated that it was very easy to fly despite its size. The cockpits were large and spacious and the big windows offered excellent visibility. By this time, because of the computerised instrumentation and avionics employed within the aircraft, the flight crew did not have to expend huge amounts of energy in order to get the aircraft into the air or keep it on course. This was in sharp contrast to their counterparts who had flown the largest aircraft in use during the 1930s.

The excellent fuel efficiency of the Boeing 747 helped to bring down the cost of flying, enabling the price of tickets to remain low and allowing more people to fly. Since 1945 the International Air Transport Association (IATA) had regulated various aspects of air travel, including fares. In the 1970s, however, this system was relaxed and highly competitive prices for international routes were introduced. A number of new airlines were established, increasing the competition. Sir Freddie Laker, the millionaire entrepreneur and pioneer of low-cost airlines, founded his company, Skytrain, in 1977. This offered tickets from London to New York for just £59. These could not be booked in advance and had to be bought on the day of travel from the company's offices. They were very popular, and queues of people trying to obtain the cheap tickets were regularly seen at the offices. Many were disappointed or had to try several times, as demand outstripped the capacity available. On board, customers found conditions spartan; meals were available, but at extra cost. This appears to have been acceptable to those flying with the airline, however, as it was the opportunity and experience of flying abroad that were important. But for customers wanting to undertake an independent short-haul journey, prices continued to be costly as these routes were expensive for the airlines to run. However, the package-tour deals available from some charter companies such as BEA's Airtours or Dan Air enabled many to enjoy the sun for less than a week's pay.

Timetable for Dan Air's Channel Islands service, and the form that was completed for the inclusive tours.

During the 1970s the passenger experience changed, but there was also an impact on the countries to which the flights went. With over six

Chaos reigns in one of the terminal buildings at Heathrow Airport during a walkout by engineers that caused delays and cancellations to flights.

million people flying all over the world, package holidays were a major contribution to the mass tourism of the period. New resorts, hotels and restaurants sprang up on various Mediterranean islands, for example, to cater for visitors. As airports struggled to cope with the vast numbers of people passing through them, many passengers experienced an increase in problems, delays and staff strikes.

One service to buck the trend of cheap commercial air travel was that provided by Concorde. This revolutionary aircraft was the result of a successful British and French collaborative project involving the aviation manufacturing companies Sud-Aviation, Aérospatiale, British Aircraft Corporation (BAC), SNECNA and Rolls Royce. This elegant, exciting and beautiful aircraft was the world's fastest passenger aircraft. It flew its first fare-paying passengers in January 1976. British Airways, which had been formed in 1973 with the merger of BOAC and BEA, flew customers from Heathrow to Bahrain, while Air France flew passengers from Paris to Rio de Janeiro. Travelling at supersonic speed (greater than that of sound) and reaching Mach 2.2, Concorde was envisaged as the future of air travel, but its commercial success was limited.

Early in its career, environmental concerns were cited as the reason for the banning of Concorde from using American airports. Although the manufacturers received a lot of interest from various airline companies during production, many decided not to buy the aircraft. The 1970s was a time of economic difficulty, and the airlines were reluctant to embrace the vision and the huge financial investment that Concorde represented. Air France and British Airways remained its main operators, with only fourteen planes in service. Like the airships of the 1930s, Concorde offered a unique flying experience at huge cost and catered for a specialised market. It could carry ninety to a hundred passengers in first-class accommodation, with seats arranged in pairs on either side of a central aisle. Tickets cost the same as the average British annual income of the period. Its main clientele was the rich and famous.

Flying at supersonic speeds created its own issues. A special heat exchange device had to be designed so that the cabin temperature could be kept at a comfortable level. Passengers found that the cabin windows were smaller than those they would have experienced on other aircraft. This was a safety measure in case the cabin lost pressure. However, customers were still able to see the curvature of the earth out of the windows during their flight, and this was no doubt one of the highlights of the trip. Customised dishes and cutlery were made specially for Concorde, designed to fit the particular tray used to serve the passengers with their food. Two things are striking about the interior of Concorde: how small the cabin was, and the fact that its furnishings were quite basic. There was none of the Pullman richness that was to be found on board 1930s luxury aircraft. Nevertheless, the service provided to customers and the whole experience of flying at supersonic speeds have been described as a once-in-a-lifetime opportunity. Concorde certainly captured the imagination of the public, and the aircraft has a unique place in air travel. It has yet to be surpassed and the decision to withdraw it from service after a series of tragic crashes and the impact on services following the attacks on the World Trade Centre in September 2001 was met with great sadness. When the final flights took place in 2003, a chapter in the history of passenger travel effectively closed.

The elegant but simple interior of Concorde's passenger cabin.

EPILOGUE

Iᴺ ᴊᴜsᴛ sɪxᴛʏ ʏᴇᴀʀs there were huge developments in air travel that have led to the passenger experience of today. The small 'stick and string' aircraft evolved into huge jumbo jets. The first people who could afford the expensive novelty of flying did so in the company of three or four other passengers and in extreme comfort, whereas today flying is no longer the preserve of the wealthy. With the low-cost airlines offering basic, cramped conditions, but bargain fares, more passengers than ever before

A De Havilland
DH18 of
AT&T, 1919.

are able to fly to most countries in the world, and they frequently do so in the company of hundreds of other people. Flying may have lost its glamour and sense of adventure as it has become an everyday activity, with the focus on the destination rather than the journey, but air travel continues to hold a strong appeal for many.

An easyJet aircraft
viewed from
an airport
waiting area.

FURTHER READING

Bennett, Air Vice-Marshal Donald. *Pathfinder*. Frederick Muller Ltd, 1958.

Coombs, L. F. E. *Control in the Sky: The Evolution and History of the Aircraft Cockpit*. Pen & Sword Aviation, 2005.

Curnock, David. *The Little Book of Concorde*. Green Umbrella Publishing, 2007.

Davies, R. E. G. *A History of the World's Airlines*. Oxford University Press, 1964.

Davies, R. E. G. *British Airways – An Airline and its Aircraft. Volume 1: 1919–1939. The Imperial Years*. Paladwr Press, 2005.

Davies, R. E. G., and Birtles, Philip. *De Havilland Comet: The World's First Jet Airliner*. Paladwr Press, 1999.

Escolme-Schmidt, Libbie. *Glamour in the Skies: The Golden Age of the Air Stewardess*. The History Press, 2009.

Gilchrist, Peter. *Boeing 747*. Ian Allan Ltd, 1985.

Harrison, James. *Mastering the Sky: A History of Aviation from Ancient Times to the Present*. Da Capo Press, 2000.

Hudson, Kenneth. *Air Travel: A Social History*. Adams & Dart, 1972.

Hudson, Kenneth, and Pettifer, Julian. *Diamonds in the Sky: Social History of Air Travel*. The Bodley Head Ltd, 1979.

Ministry of Information. *Merchant Airmen: The Air Ministry Account of British Civil Aviation, 1939–1944*. His Majesty's Stationery Office, 1946.

Prior, Rupert. *Flying – The Golden Years: A Pictorial Anthology*. H. C. Blossom Ltd, 1991.

Smith, Graham. *Taking to the Skies: The Story of British Aviation, 1903–1939*. Countryside Books, 2003.

Woods, Eric. *From Flying Boats to Flying Jets: Flying in the Formative Years of BOAC, 1946–1971*. Airlife, 1997.

PLACES TO VISIT

British Airways Heritage Collection, Waterside (HDGA), PO Box 365,
  Harmondsworth, Middlesex UB7 0GB. Telephone: 020 8562 5777.
  Website: www.britishairways.com/travel/museum-collection

Brooklands Museum, Brooklands Road, Weybridge, Surrey KT13 0QN.
  Telephone: 01932 857381. Website: www.brooklandsmuseum.com

Croydon Airport Visitor Centre, Airport House, Purley Way, Croydon CR0 0XZ.
  Telephone: 020 8669 1196. Website: www.croydonairport.org.uk

Fleet Air Arm Museum, RNAS Yeovilton, Ilchester, Somerset BA22 8HT.
  Telephone: 01935 840565. Website: www.fleetairarm.com

Imperial War Museum Duxford, Cambridgeshire CB22 4QR. Telephone:
  01223 835000. Website: www.iwm.org.uk

National Museum of Flight, East Fortune Airfield, East Lothian EH39 5LF.
  Telephone: 030 0123 6789. Website: www.nms.ac.uk

Royal Air Force Museum, Grahame Park Way, Hendon, London NW9 5LL.
  Telephone: 020 8205 2266. Website: www.rafmuseum.org.uk

Royal Air Force Museum Cosford, Shifnal, Shropshire TF11 8UP. Telephone:
  01902 376200. Website: www.rafmuseum.org.uk

Science Museum, Exhibition Road, South Kensington, London SW7 2DD.
  Telephone: 0870 8704868. Website: www.sciencemuseum.org.uk

The Shuttleworth Collection, Shuttleworth (Old Warden) Aerodrome, near
  Biggleswade, Bedfordshire SG18 9EP. Telephone: 01767 627927.
  Website: www.shuttleworth.org

Solent Sky Museum, 7 Albert Road South, Southampton, Hampshire SO14
  3FR. Telephone: 023 8063 5830. Website: www.spitfireonline.co.uk

INDEX

Page numbers in italics refer to illustrations

Airco 9
Aircraft
  Aérospatiale-BAC
    Concorde 50, 51, *51*
  Airbus 300: 47
  Airspeed Oxford *26*
  Armstrong Whitworth
    Argosy 13
  Armstrong Whitworth
    AW27 Ensign 16, *16*
  Atlantia 6, 7
  Avro Lancastrian 29
  Avro Tudor C5: *28*, 29
  Avro York 29
  Boeing 307 Stratoliner 29
  Boeing 314 Flying Boat
    26, *26*
  Boeing 707: 39, 40
  Boeing 747: 47–9, *48*
  Boeing Stratocruiser *32*,
    33, 34
  Bristol Britannia 33, 34
  British Aircraft
    Corporation BAC
    111: 40
  Charabanc (Grahame-
    White Type 10): *9*
  De Havilland Comet *32*,
    38, 39, 39, 40, *41*
  De Havilland DH18: 11,
    53, *53*
  De Havilland DH34: 11
  De Havilland DH89
    Dragon Rapide 22, *22*
  De Havilland Mosquito
    27, *27*
  Douglas DC-10: 47
  Douglas DC-3 Dakota
    24, 25, *25*
  Douglas DC-4: *32*, 33,
    37, *37*
  Douglas DC-6: 33
  Fokker VII: 11
  Glen Martin 130: 19
  Graf Zeppelin LZ 127:
    18, 20, *20*
  Graf Zeppelin LZ 129
    Hindenburg 19
  Handley Page Hermes
    32, 33, 36, *36*
  Handley Page HP42: 15,
    16, *16*, 17, *17*
  Handley Page HP66: 13
  Handley Page O/400: *9*
  Handley Page W8A 11, *12*
  Hawker Siddeley
    HS748: 47
  Hawker Siddeley Trident
    40, 47
  Junkers F.13: 12
  Junkers Ju 52: 38, *38*
  Lockheed Constellation
    29, *32*, 33, 34, *34*
  Lockheed Electra 23, *23*
  Lockheed Tristar 47
  Royal Airship Works
    R101: 19
  Short S.23 Empire Class
    20, *20–1*
  Sud Caravelle 39
  Tupolov Tu-104: 39
  Vickers VC-10: 40
  Vickers Viscount 33,
    41, *41*
Air France 25, 39, 42, *42*,
  50, 51
Air India 44
Air Mail 8
Air shows/Aerial derbies 7
Air traffic control 28
Air Transport Auxiliary 26,
  26, 27
Aircraft Transport and Travel
  (AT&T) 9, 10, 53, *53*
Airport facilities 11, 29, *30–
  1*, *41*, 45, 50, *50*
Airships 7, *18*, 19, *19*, 51
Balloonists 7, *8*
Bennett, Capt Donald 27
Boeing Air Transport 15
Bray, Capt Alan DFC 29, *29*,
  36, 42, *42*
British Airways (BA) 23, 24,
  48, *48*, 50, 51
British European Airways
  (BEA) 28, 37, *37*, 38,
  38, 40, 45, 49, 50
British Marine Air
  Navigation Company
  (BMAN) 12
British Overseas Aircraft
  Corporation (BOAC) 24,
  25, 27, *27*, 28, 29, *32*,
  33, 34, *35*, 36, 37, *37*,
  41, 50
British South American
  Airways (BSAA) 28,
  28, 29
Cabin decor 11, 12, *12*, 15,
  16, *16*, 19, 21, 34, 43,
  44, 51, *51*
Cardington airship sheds
  19, *19*
Chamberlain, Neville 23, *23*
Channel Island Airways 23
Church, Ms Ellen 15
Churchill, Sir Winston 25,
  26, *26*, 27
Classes of travel 12, 37, 40,
  41, 47
Cobham, Sir Alan 18, 22
Cockpits 12, 17, *17*, 26, 38,
  38, 49
Communications equipment
  12, 27, 42
Crews
  Air stewardesses/hostesses
    15, 17, *32*, 36, *37*,
    40–2, *41*, *42*, 44, 47,
    48, *48*
  Air stewards/hosts 13,
    13, 15, *41*, 47
  First officers 12
  Navigators 28
  Pay and conditions 10, 12
  Pilots 7, 10, 12, *26*, 36, 49
  Radio operators 18
Refreshments 36
Cricklewood, London 9
Croydon Airport 6, 7, 11, 29
Daimler Airway 11, *11*, 12
Dan Air 37, 49, *49*
Da Vinci, Leonardo 5
Deutsche Luft Reederei 8
Easyjet *52–3*, 53
Fares 7, 10, 11, 12, 19, 21,
  22, 37, 40, 49, 51
Flying boats *14*, 15, 19, 20,
  21, 26, 26, 28
Gatwick 22
Gibraltar 25, *25*
Glamour of flight 5, 7, 10,
  12, 13, 15, 36, 40, *43*, 53
Grahame-White Aviation
  Company Limited 7
Grahame-White, Claude 9
Hambling Committee 12
Handley Page Transport 10,
  12
Hayes, Wg Off 25, 27
Heathrow 28, 29, *30–1*, 41,
  41, *43*, 48, *50*
Hendon 7, *8*, 9
Heston 23
Hillman Airways 23
Hounslow Heath 10, 11
Howard, Leslie 24
Icarus 5
Imperial Airways *4*, 5, 7, 12,
  13, 17, *17*, 18, 19, 21,
  22, 23, 24, 40
Instone Air Line Limited 12
International Air Transport
  Association (IATA) 49
Koninklijke Luchtvaart
Maatschappij NV (KLM)
  12, 18
Laker, Freddie *46*, 49
Laker Airways 47
Le Bourget 10
Lindbergh, Charles 19
Lisbon 24
London-Paris air route 9,
  10, 13, *13*
Long haul flights 18, 19, 21,
  24, 27, 28, 37
Lufthansa 8, 12, 24, 38
Luton 22
Maybury Committee 22–3
Ocean liners 11, 15
Pan American Airways (Pan
  Am) 19, 39
Passenger
  Comfort 10, 11, 12, 15,
    16, *16*, 17, 18, 19, 20,
    20, 21, 22, 27, *27*, 29,
    32, 33, 34, 37, 38, 40,
    42, 43, 47, 49, 52
  Entertainments 28, 43,
    44, 47
  Facilities 10, 15, *17*, 18,
    20, *20*, 21, 22, 24, 27,
    32, 34, 36, 43, 45, *45*,
    47, 51
  Refreshments 10, 13, *13*,
    15, *32*, 34, 36, *41*, 42,
    43, 44, *44*, 49, 51
  Safety 10, 12, 17, 21, 24,
    27, *27*
  Weighing *11*
Pressurised cabins 29, 33
Qantas 18
Rail travel 11, 15
Railway Air Services *22*, 23
Ringway (Manchester) 22
Royal Air Force 27, 28, 29
Schiphol (Amsterdam) 11
'Silver Wing' service
  (Imperial Airways) 13, *13*
Skytrain (airline) 49
Spartan Airlines 23
Speke (Liverpool) 22,
Stewart, Lt Col Charles
  Edward 7
United Air Lines 15
United Airways 23
Vienna *8*
Western Airways *22*
Women's Auxiliary Air
  Force 27
Woods, Flt Lt Eric 28
Wunstorf 28, *28*